Table of Contents

Introduction
Page 4

The Toolbox: 55 Ways to Connect With Your Kids
Page 6

101 Fun and Safe Things You Can Do With Kids
Page 115

Questions to Ask Kids
Page 120

Things To Surprise Your Kids
Page 123

Other Resources
Page 125

About the Author
Page 127

Having A Presence In Your Absence

Having A Presence In Your Absence

How to be there even when you can't!

A Guide for Busy Dads

Derek G. Carter

Having A Presence
In Your Absence

How to be there even when you can't!
A Guide for Busy Dads

Derek G. Carter

Copyright © 2005, 2011 (2nd Edition) by Derek Carter

Cover design by Jolene Carter
Book design by Jarrett Carter
Editing by Janaé Carter

All rights reserved.
No part of this book may be reproduced in any form or by any electronic or mechanical means including information storage and retrieval systems, without permission in writing from the author. The only exception is by a reviewer, who may quote short excerpts in a review.
Printed in the United States of America

ISBN-13: 978-0-9818417-5-5
ISBN 10: 0-9818417-5-9

Published by:
Family Success Publications
PO Box 712
Uniondale, New York 11553-0712
www.familysuccess.org

Thank You

Thank you to my LORD and Savior Jesus Christ for blessing me with the opportunity and privilege to be a father.

Introduction

Okay, so I'm not going to waste any time. I am going to get right to the point. All of us know we should be spending more time with our kids and that time should be meaningful. The problem for most of us is by the time when we finish working at the office, or perhaps getting back from a long deployment, the desire to be with our kids is there but what to do with them becomes the question. "What to do?" is further complicated by our lack of planning. Yes, we know we want to be with the kids, but just what do we do?

We want to be more than just a substitute for mom. No father wants to feel like a hired hand. We want to impact our families in such a meaningful way that when we are not physically there, our presence is still felt. We want to have a presence in our absence. I am going to make certain assumptions. First, I'm going to assume you are a busy dad. There is probably not one of us who isn't busy these days. I am also going to assume that like me, you want to spend more time with your kids but are not really sure what to do. This is just the book to help you make connections. The fact is when you connect with your children in a meaningful way it has a lasting effect that transcends the time spent. After all, what is a memory but an activity or event in time pressed fondly upon the mind. As dads, we have to work hard to make memories because we can get so caught up in providing financially and "tomorrow-thinking" for our families that we miss the opportunity to connect today.

Today is most important for our kids. It has been said that kids spell love, "T-I-M-E." Hmmm, I think it was my wife that told me that. We want our kids to get older and say "remember when..." and recall all the good times. I know that as a man and a dad I should be spending more time with our kids, but sometimes balancing the checkbook calls louder than the baseball glove gathering dust in a corner.

Our kids need us today.

Now I'm not here to lay a guilt trip on you because I understand. The issue is having a plan of what you can do with the kids. This is a practical guide of fifty-five ideas and/or activities that you can do with your kids.

Derek G. Carter

The Toolbox

55 Ways To Connect With Your Kids

1
Write Letters To Your Kids

> This is why I write these things when I am absent, that when I come I may not have to be harsh in my use of authority—the authority the Lord gave me for building you up, not for tearing you down.
> - 2 Corinthians 13:10 (NIV)

Paul wrote his thoughts down to prepare the Corinthian church for his return. Paul seems to indicate he was writing on some harsh topics. We should never write harsh things to our children. When we need to confront them on issues it should be done face-to-face in loving conversations.

Nonetheless, we learn a principle from Paul here. Writing is a way of impacting your children and you don't have to be a poet to write to your children, because they are not critics.

Write brief letters to your children. This is one of the easiest ways to be there when you cannot. You do not have to be gifted with words to write because children just appreciate the effort. You can put them under their pillow, in their lunch box or slip it in their coat pocket. My children are home schooled and so I occasionally hide them around the house for them to find. Of course, I sometimes have to write down where I put them myself because when my wife calls me at work so many things are on my mind that I am apt to forget where I put them.

The letters do not have to be so sentimental. I like writing funny letters to the kids or asking them silly or challenging questions (See suggested questions in the Appendix) that they have to think about.

Sometimes I encourage them to ask me questions and they give me letters too. In this way, I keep them thinking about me. When I walk through the door at night, they are anticipating my arrival and we all can quickly make an emotional connection.

By having a common and shared reference point, conversation is easily initiated. My children also like to hold onto my letters. You may buy your kids a special storage box or you can make a box out of an old shoe box as a project together.

Writing letters to your family really impacts them because when you write, you give a piece of yourself. It is also a tangible memory kids can return to even as adults to recall the time they have spent with you.

2
Read to Your Kids

> That night the king could not sleep; so he ordered the book of the chronicles, the record of his reign, to be brought in and read to him.
> - Esther 6:1 (NIV)

Reading is very comforting. Reading helps with our thinking process. In this passage of scripture, God used a book to remind the king of Israel's history and faithfulness. Because the book was read the nation of Israel was spared. God used a book and a sleepless night to redeem a whole nation.

Pick a good book and read to your children. I still like reading hardcover classic children's books to my kids. Brief books with long term meaning are best if your time is limited or if you can carve out time in the evening, a novel is best. Older children still like having books read to them like "The Giving Tree" by Sheldon Silverstein. Ravi Zacharias Ministries has tremendous theologically sound and inspiring hardcover books with timeless messages that spark conversation. You can also read classic books in a children's version if you prefer. We have read Shakespearean children's editions and other children's classics such as Homer's Odyssey. By reading the children's version our children are exposed to the ideas and will be better able to understand the more complex concepts later as they get older. There are also good Christian children's books which embrace character qualities you may want your children to emulate.

I have discussed values and ideas with my children that many would have considered beyond their understanding. I did this by simply asking questions. Do you agree with the decision the main character made? Why or why not?

Can you think of a better biblical response? Simple questions like this spur a child to think and it gently allows me to probe their thinking in a way that is not threatening, because I am not lecturing them directly about something they have or have not done. It affords me the opportunity to really mold their decision making process.

We have also read books about missionaries and famous Americans when they were young. Our kids seem to enjoy discovering things about famous people when they were children. They relate well to these kinds of books and it fosters conversation about what they want to do in the future. Biographies that are well written are excellent. In my own spiritual journey I have enjoyed reading many different authors. It is important that our children understand our rich spiritual heritage.

As the scripture text indicates when we are read to then we are comforted. Reading to your child will also help bedtimes to be more peaceful and also develops your child's vocabulary as well as the love of reading. Isn't it great to know we can impact our family just by opening up a book?

You can also set a goal for reading the Bible through in a specified time and read it with your children. You can easily find read the bible through in one year plans. There are various methods. Here is one of several links for one year bible reading: http://www.bible-reading.com/bible-plan.html.

3
Family Chapel

> Gather the people, consecrate the assembly; bring together the elders, gather the children, those nursing at the breast...
> - Joel 2:16a (NIV)

At important times in Israel's history, God summoned all the people together, even the children, for worship. In this scripture the prophet Joel also indicates that infants should be included. Worship time included entire families. Traditionally, most of us think church is the only place to worship but you can also have a time of ministry with your family at home. We call it Family Chapel.

Family Chapel is when we as a family read the Bible, sing worship songs and generally hear a brief message of biblical encouragement. Typically, I as the dad generally lead our family worship sessions although I occasionally alternate with my wife at her request. However, as our children have gotten older I encourage them to take turns studying the bible and teaching a clear biblical message to the rest of the family.

Generally, when the children lead bible study they will imitate me and come to me with questions as they are preparing for Family Chapel. We plan Family Chapel on a weekly and occasionally on a bi-weekly basis. Family Chapel is fun for us. At times we imitate a church service but over the years it has evolved into an activity where each of us is encouraged to practice teaching, exhortation, and our musical abilities.

Your Family Chapel will be different based on your family size, denomination and purpose. We keep Family Chapel strictly focused on the LORD Jesus. We come together collectively to worship our Lord and to offer to Him our worship. We generally have a time of praise and worship and then Bible study. We do attend a local church and are very active in our local church but we find

Family Chapel solidifies our children's biblical foundation as well as their family foundation.

When you have Family Chapel you can correct any doctrinal errors and fill in the gaps of your child's biblical knowledge. In addition to your teaching them, once they are given the opportunity to teach Family Chapel it solidifies their scriptural knowledge. What better way to impact your family then to help them understand their faith better?

4
Family Meetings

> "Come now, let us reason together," says the LORD....
> -Isaiah. 1:18a (NIV)

God invites us here to a meeting to reason together. A time to reason together is part of the way our Heavenly Father deals with us and it is the way we can deal with our children. A meeting is the place where we come to make decisions and to move forward in our group goals.

We occasionally have family meetings. Anyone can call a family meeting. They are generally called to resolve conflict. I use the family meetings to reinforce our family rules, rehearse our family mission statement, and to foster family togetherness. We generally keep it to a specified time session and with a definite agenda, lest it degenerate into a griping session. We used to have weekly family meetings when our children were young. We used the meetings to remind our children of the rules and to reaffirm our family's code of conduct both in and out the home. Now that our children are older, we have them only on an as needed basis.

We find it works best if you take a timer to the meeting and give family members a specified time to express their opinion so that the meetings do not run excessively long.

Knowing they have a time limit helps preschoolers and toddlers to think through their ideas instead of just rambling.

This will not eliminate their random thoughts but will help move the meeting along and eventually youngsters (and parents too) will realize they have to think through their thoughts before coming to the meeting, especially if meetings are called due to specific areas. My wife and I tend to call meetings when the home is getting messy, (and the kids have learned to just pick up a bit to avoid the meeting).

Family meetings communicate to your children that you want to hear them. It also impacts their hearts to know their opinions are important to you.

5
Provide Mentors

> The king answered the people harshly. Rejecting the advice given him by the elders, he followed the advice of the young men.
> - 1 Kings 12:13-14 (NIV)

If you have read the account of the reign of Rehoboam, you know this dynasty ended in disaster because he refused to listen to the advice of the elders, who were more knowledgeable than the younger men. Everyone needs mentors, those who help us in our weaknesses.

Many men struggle with admitting their weaknesses. I was never good in sports, although when people meet me they automatically assume I am either a basketball or football player because of my size and stature. I dabbled a bit in sports in college due to my roommate's interest, but overall I never developed a passion for any sport other than jogging. In addition, my schedule is so busy that I just do not have the time or the inclination to master any sport. I have noticed as a result that my son was not interested in sports. Growing up as a young man it can be a great hindrance not to have any interest in sports. So I have other men who I know and trust to mentor my son in that area.

If we want our children to play the piano we have no problem enlisting the help of a good piano teacher if we lacked those skills. We have to do the same in all the areas of our lives. This takes honesty on our part to admit our deficiencies. I think all of us have to assess our weaknesses and fill in the gap.

The idea is to identify a trusted friend with your values that can teach your child in areas you lack the necessary skill. This is an important function because it teaches the need to reach out for help. It is especially important for male children to learn the need for horizontal and vertical mentors. A vertical mentor is someone who achieved what you are still striving to accomplish. You therefore submit to someone who has already achieved something in an area you have not yet mastered. A horizontal mentor is someone that is trying to achieve the same thing you are. Therefore, you are encouraging each other.

Men tend not to reach out for help as easily as women do. It is really not as hard as it may sound. In fact, you can have your friend teach you and your child at the same time. We can grow in this area with our children at the same time. For example, when I sit down to watch a football game with my son, we are both learning about the game.

Allowing our children to see our weaknesses and shortcomings and to also watch us grow in those areas impacts them in ways we cannot fully fathom. It also teaches our children that it is okay to make mistakes and that it is never too late to learn something new. So when we model humility before them by securing good mentors, we too grow in the process and are likewise impacted.

6
Memorable Bible Study

> You diligently study the Scriptures because you think that by them you possess eternal life. These are the Scriptures that testify about me.
> - John 5:39 (NIV)

It is important that we study the Bible. Certainly, we know that. Our relationship rests on our knowledge and understanding of our Creator Jesus Christ. The scriptures are our life. Bible study is pivotal to our spiritual growth.

We need to have a brief time to sit down with our children and show them how to study the Bible. We are thus giving them a life skill. I sit down with my children and explain how to use the bible concordance, find the books of the bible and how to approach a scripture that pertains to a certain issue.

God has to be real to our children. This may seem very minimal to most men but our children need to go to the LORD for their answers first and when we give them basic bible study skills we are giving them life skills.

When we have brief bible studies with our kids and ask them questions about the Bible we are fostering in them a love for scripture particularly when we do it in a fun and emotionally bonding way.

It is important to realize that children generally remember incidents and experiences by their own perceptions. I once remembered going down a slide that seemed enormous when I was a kid. When I visited that same playground as an adult the slide seemed very small. When I pointed that out to my wife, who has studied child development, she informed me that most childhood memories are framed by a child's emotional response to the event or an activity and not necessarily the activity itself. Therefore, we should make bible study fun and memorable for our children. We can ask meaningful and emotionally charged questions like, "What do you think you would have done if you were Joseph?"

You may even encourage your child to dress up like a bible character and come to bible study as such. The important thing to do is to make it memorable. We are preparing our children in bible study to make critical decisions when we will not be there to answer questions.

It is also important that you get your child a Bible they can read. Our children studied from the New International Readers Version when they first began to study on their own. It was easy for them to read and understand that version. We make it a ceremony in our family for each child to get their own Bible. You can do the same.

There are many family devotional books. See my suggestions in the Appendix. The Bible is a book that we receive greater revelation each time we read it. God speaks in His word. By giving our children a love for the Scripture we are helping them to connect with God.

7
Schedule Brief Talk Times

> When I called, you answered me...
> - Psalm 138:3 (NIV)

It is the nature of God to answer us when we call. We are parenting our children the way the Father God parents us.

We should make time or rather schedule times when they can call us so we will be able to answer them.

On my job I am constantly getting calls. Usually when the telephone rings I know it is someone with a problem. However, in the afternoon, which tends to be my down time, I will telephone the kids or have them telephone me individually. Practically, I cannot do this everyday but I can on occasion telephone them individually. I will generally ask them how their day is going or did they get a note I wrote to them. It is important for me to speak to them individually and alternate the times of the call so each individual child feels special.

I only have three children and I realize it is easier for me than dads with more children but you can limit the duration of the time you speak to each child or ask each one a different question. This works well if you ask a silly question. See my list of silly questions at the end of this book.

It is especially important to plan times when your kids can call you particularly if you tend to get busy or preoccupied with things at work. If you cannot telephone them, perhaps email will work for you. You can also send free e-cards to your children. Many websites have animated and funny childlike e-cards. In this way, the Internet can be used to enhance your relationship with your child.

Dads, it is vitally important that we keep our scheduled time to talk to our kids. The talks do not necessarily have to be long, they just have to be frequent. Our children need to know we keep our promises so do not schedule a time to talk with your children without checking your calendar for appointments. Children can accept a disappointment now and then but when you continually break your promise to them a kind of staunch cynicism sets in that is difficult to deal with even when they are adults.

By being available to our children we impact them because we teach them they should always ask questions because an answer is not far from them. We also likewise teach them that godly Fathers like their heavenly Fathers answer when they call.

8
Make Goals With your Child

> The plans of the diligent lead to profit as surely as haste leads to poverty.
> - Proverbs 21:5 (NIV)

It is vital that we teach our children the value of hard work by helping them make goals and then diligently pursuing those goals. Sit with your children and have each child make a goal. The goal should be something the child wants to do and try not to censor the goal. For instance, my seven year old wanted to learn how to ride a skateboard. She was watching older kids and much to my surprise my darling little girl really wanted to learn to skateboard. First we got her the skateboard. I must point out this was no easy task because most skateboards were designed for teen riders in addition were just too masculine for my little girl.

Then I got her a helmet, knee guards and arm guards. I resisted the urge to get her body padding and also relented and allowed her to skateboard on asphalt. We did a bit of research and wrote down everything she needed to do to skateboard successfully. This sheet became her progress sheet.

Occasionally I would ask her how she was doing. I would like to say I asked her daily but sometimes I did forget. At times I would watch her skateboarding and give her a few tips. She never thought to ask me how I was qualified to give her advice when I didn't know how to do it myself. I still relish in my children's undying love and faith in me. At times the responsibility to be so much to them is weighty. At other times I am just so grateful to the LORD for the gift of children. Of course, as they approach their teenage or transitional years they are more prone to question my ability to advise them on matters of importance so I continue to enjoy the moment now.

Generally, when I make goals with the kids I leave my wife out of the equation for several reasons: first I really want to connect with my kids on a personal basis and when they make a goal with me it feels like we are working on it together. Second, and more importantly, my wife probably would not agree with the goal. She still does not see the value in my daughter skateboarding but I know her success at learning to skateboard has translated into her success in home-school and other areas. The same goal setting skills are required no matter what she does. Reading the Bible through in a whole year is also a great goal to work on with your kids. And if you are like me, the competition keeps you on your toes too.

By helping my kids set goals, I teach them that they are not hindered by the past or their present and that diligence has its own reward. They are also impacted because they learn they can affect their destinies.

9
Share Stories

> ...that you may tell your children and grandchildren how I dealt harshly with the Egyptians and how I performed my signs among them, and that you may know that I am the LORD.
> - Exodus 10:2 b (NIV)

In this passage God gives a command. He tells the children of Israel to tell the story of how He delivered them from the Egyptians. A good story captivates children especially when they know the characters.

I think the greatest way I can give my kids a piece of myself is to share stories about myself. I think it gives them the opportunity to connect with me and know that I am human. The way your child views their relationship with you will influence how they view their relationship with their heavenly Father. I want to be a bridge to their heavenly Father and not a moat so I want to be real with them. Fathers tend to appear as this huge authority figure.

Children sometimes cannot imagine their fathers as children. It is important that our children are able to visualize us as children, to know that we once felt the same feelings, inadequacies and fear of making mistakes they are feeling.

Sharing stories will help diminish the perception that dad is such an inapproachable giant. I have shared how I flooded our family apartment, received well-earned spankings and my little boy antics. My children prefer to hear my stories than regular bedtime stories. God never wastes anything. He even had the disciples pick up the scraps of bread after he feed the disciples. God continues to pick up the scraps of my life by my sharing stories with my children. Your past experiences can become humorous stories and teachable lessons for your children.

Jesus taught primarily using stories. He did it perhaps because he knew a good story may minister to the mind but generally crosses over to the heart.

10
Daily Time With Each Child

> When he was alone, the Twelve and the others around him asked him about the parables.
> - Mark 4:10 (NIV)

Jesus took time to be alone with his disciples. At times Jesus spent time alone praying to the Father. He understood the value of personal one-on-one time. All children like to know they are valued so I try to spend a little bit of time with each child individually. Since bedtime is staggered in our home, I find it easy to do this at bedtime. I ask them individually about their day. Since my children are home schooled, occasionally they will also register their complaints about their mom or other siblings. I listen and pray with the child. I rarely lecture or give a solution unless I see the child is really looking for an answer.

Most times I find my children just want to vent. Once their feelings are validated by me acknowledging their feelings, and they see their feelings are justified then I can easily help them release their offenses. I once read that feelings are not right or wrong. Feelings are caused by thoughts. So when a child seems to be very angry, sad or fearful I try to get them to tell me what they were thinking which led to that feeling.

Once I correct their thinking by challenging the wrong thoughts, they generally will feel better. A good book to read on this technique is "Teaching Your Child to Tell the Truth" by Dr. Backus. Dr. Backus is a Lutheran counselor who has had a high degree of success teaching people to replace negative thoughts with Scripture and what God says about you. I have used this method in counseling adults and find it is quite effective with children as well.

Children feel validated when we take the time to be alone with them. Jesus explained the parables to his disciples when He was alone. We can use the time to explain why we disciplined them or why we believe what we believe. It can also be a time to talk about what is on your child's heart. If the time is planned daily, your children will not starve for attention. This time should be brief yet meaningful.

11
Daddy and Me Day

> Do two walk together unless they have agreed to do so?
> - Amos 3:3 (NIV)

Agreement is something we rarely think about as fathers. We want our kids to agree with us but we rarely give them the opportunity to express themselves and what is important to them. We have to engage them to find out their likes and dislikes. This can only be done by spending time with your child.

In our home we have seasonal "Daddy and Me" Days. On these Saturdays, each child gets to choose whatever s/he wants to do for the day. Instead of the child shadowing me and adhering to my schedule, I give them a day to choose whatever they want to do.

I started to do this because I realized some divorced parents were spending more time with their kids than those from two parent homes. I also realized that on many weekends I had my own agenda and my kids were just my shadow but not really doing things they enjoyed. I started doing it also to connect individually with each child. You can alter this idea by taking a child out to breakfast or a special meal.

Daddy and Me Days are not expensive or very elaborate. For instance, my thirteen year old son wanted to go to the car dealer on his day. My middle daughter wanted to go to the bookstore where they have an extensive children's section. Other dates have been bike riding, playing in the park and teaching Daddy to skateboard. The important thing is that you give the child the choice about what to do for the day. Originally, I tried to do it monthly but given my speaking, work, and church schedule it was not feasible. Now we do it quarterly. You can do it monthly so each child gets a month if you have a large family.

You can adapt the concept to work for you. You may have a morning your child spends with you, or an evening after work. It is imperative that the child decides on the activity. You may want to set a price limit if your child is prone to choose expensive activities. The idea is to discover something about your child and do it with him.

12
Do Projects Together

> He carried into exile all Jerusalem: all the officers and fighting men, and all the craftsmen and artisans—a total of ten thousand. Only the poorest people of the land were left.
> - 2 Kings 24:14 (NIV)

Nebuchadnezzar knew the value of craftsmen so much so that he carried them off when he captured Israel. Craftspeople were highly valued. When you do a craft with your children you s/he not only has the memory of the experience but of working with you to accomplish a goal. Working together with your children really fosters problem solving skills.

We know a family that worked on a go-cart then they voted on which child would participate in the race. We have worked on other projects not as lofty.

Once we made a weather station in the back yard. We also include our children in on our ministry and job related projects. Working on projects with tight deadlines and high stress levels can provide real opportunities to grow our family conflict resolution skills. While we have read many books on conflict resolution and the importance of being a peace maker there is no place like real life to really enforce this life skill.

These skills will provide the child a reference point when working with others. The skills will not soon be forgotten because the skills were learned in a fun enriching environment with a desired goal.

Children remember things that are fun. Invite your kids to assist you with your home improvement projects. Instead of having a honey to-do list, change it into a family to-do list where everyone will benefit from the task getting done and the camaraderie it creates is priceless.

13
Good Habits

> Follow my example, as I follow the example of Christ.
> -1 Corinthians 11:1 (NIV)

The apostle Paul admonishes us to follow him as he follows Christ. He is our example to the degree he follows Christ. We are examples to our children to the degree we follow Christ too. Our kids watch us and will generally automatically do what we do and not necessarily what we say.

I know this seems really obvious but our children pick up our habits. I am an early riser. I encourage my kids to do likewise. We are still working on that one. Here's one where again guys we have to be honest. Our kids will imitate what we do and question what we say. They are always watching us.

Sometimes our influence is not so noticeable but it is there. My wife used to tell me when she first began home-schooling my son that she struggled to get him to read books independently. We have since realized he, like most boys, liked action and adventure and had a preference for nonfiction books. When I was a child my parents also struggled to get me to read. My mother was a school teacher. I frustrated her to no end because I did not like the books other kids typically enjoyed. As an adult I have cultivated a love of reading but it did not come naturally to me.

My son tends to be like me in his choice of reading. I'm not sure if it is in his genes as my wife tells me or if he just noticed the kinds of things I was reading. At any rate, I realized my son who identifies with me as the only male in the house will get up early like me and do the things I do. Therefore, I have to be mindful of my bad habits.

No parent likes this fact. I would like my children to form good habits yet I realize this will not happen if I don't pattern good habits before them or at least be honest and willing to change my bad habits.

14
Family Games

> They are like children sitting in the marketplace and calling out to each other: "'We played the flute for you, and you did not dance; we sang a dirge, and you did not cry.'
> - Luke 7:32 (NIV)

Jesus knew the games the little children played. He could recite their choruses. He likens the kingdom of God to little children. He knew the value of children. He often played with them. In the temple it was the children who shouted Hosanna to the highest (Matthew 21:15) Jesus put value in children. We can too by playing games with them.

Games which involve fun and strategy are best. We frequently will have a family game night. Some of our favorite games are: Monopoly, Sorry, Stratego, Guess Who, Connect Four, Life, Clue, Trouble, Cranium Cadoo, and Pictionary, Kids Battle the Grownups, Hangman, Checkers and Chess.

Board and strategy games provide a means for light hearted conversation. I especially like talking to the kids about some of the strategies I employed when I played the same games as a kid. Besides really connecting with my children, it also gives my children the opportunity to share with their friends their father's game strategy when they play the games with their friends when I am not around.

It also gives me a little time to be silly with them and to unwind from the seriousness of my day. I find being forced to enter my children's world helps me to forget the worries of the office, bills and other distractions. This is by no means an easy thing to do but I am working on letting go and letting God take control. Often He guides me into a place of peace by just simply playing with my children.

15
Family Creed

> No longer will you be called Abram; your name will be Abraham, for I have made you a father of many nations.
> - Genesis 17:5 (NIV)

Names are important to God. Abram was given the name Abraham, which means father of many nations to propagate God's promise in his life. Our name defines who we are and what is important to us.

In the army you generally give your name, rank and serial number. In our family we are developing a family creed. All Carters are honest. I am a Carter therefore I am honest. In doing this I am bringing a sense of family togetherness that will give them a sense of identity. We also have different sayings and things that only pertain to our family. The kids will often tell me when they are spending time with me what mom would or would not say about us doing something.

At first, I was a bit annoyed that they repeated what their mother would say or whether she would approve of something we were doing. Later I learned from my wife that when I am not there the children would often parrot what I would say or not say. This brings up an important point. It is ideal if both mother and father are on the same page, however if you are divorced or both parents simply parent differently, choose positive affirmations that the other parent would most likely approve of.

You can create your own family creed using Scripture. For instance, *"Blessed is the man who does not walk in the counsel of the wicked..."* Psalm 1:1 (NIV). We do not stand in the counsel of the ungodly so we are a blessed family. You can print your family creed out and display it somewhere in your home to help make it look official for the children.

16
Role Play

> So Joab sent someone to Tekoa and had a wise woman brought from there. He said to her, "Pretend you are in mourning. Dress in mourning clothes, and don't use any cosmetic lotions. Act like a woman who has spent many days grieving for the dead.
> - 2 Samuel 14:2

In the above Scripture, Joab recognizing King David's heart was breaking over Absalom has a woman pretend to be in mourning to get him (King David) to deal with the issue of his grief of having Absalmon banished for killing his brother Abijah to avenge the rape of his sister. Of course, King David relents and has his son Absalom return. He is moved by the role play of this woman. Role playing, or simply pretending to be someone else can offer great insight into your child.

I like to switch roles with my children and allow them to pretend to be the adults. This works well for a brief time and play has to cease when my son asks me for the car keys. Still I have found role play to be a great way to see how kids view things. It can open the door for meaningful conversation. Role play is best done when done in realistic situations. For instance, if your family is late for church you might later on switch roles and then act out what happened on Sunday morning.

You might be really surprised. Our children are really adept at imitating us. We have to be ready to repent and that means to genuinely change our behavior if we discover we are too harsh when our kids role play us. I work in a high stress job dealing with families in continual crisis and have to really work on being there for my family when I come through the door. I work really hard on this and just seeing my kids role play me is a powerful word picture for me that really provokes me to change.

17
Teach A Topic

> Jesus then left that place and went into the region of Judea and across the Jordan. Again crowds of people came to him, and as was his custom, he taught them.
> - Mark 10:1 (NIV)

Jesus took the time to teach his disciples. There are times when we have to stop and teach our children. We dads are sometimes good at lecturing our children but sometimes we are quick to correct our children when in reality we have never taught them the right thing to do. Correction can only be provided after we teach. We have to make the time to teach what we want them to learn. If we want them to manage money we have to teach money management skills, if we want them to get along better with their siblings we have to teach conflict resolution skills.

There are many ways to teach. Since our children are home educated I assist my wife by teaching a subject. I love history in particular the sixties. As a result my children know many of the people, events and political underpinnings of that period in history. I try to expose my kids to the things I love.

Generally, we think they would not be interested in what interests us. This is just not true. If you are passionate about something, then it is rather easy to convey that passion to others. I share my political views and give them concrete reasons why I believe what I believe. Also it is important that we convey our Christian values to the next generation.

Our children need to be able to understand and defend their Christian faith. I encourage them to be able to historically and biblically document the deity of Jesus Christ and the inerrancy of scripture. I do this by sharing with them historic facts and information from books that I have read. My wife also is good at documenting our family spiritual journey through things like a spiritual journal with answered family prayers.

18
Mission Statement

> Where there is no revelation, the people cast off restraint; but blessed is he who keeps the law.
> - Proverbs 29:15 (NIV)

A mission statement is the revelation of our lives because it directs us where we are going. It is the vision for our lives. Vision is used to implement strategy. The development of strategy is driven by what you are trying to accomplish. Your vision should be realistic, credible, well articulated and easily understood, further it should be appropriate, ambitious and responsive to change.

When we think of writing a mission statement we often think of having one for corporate companies or large organizations but the family is the most important group on the globe therefore every family should have one. Our mission statement is simple so the kids can understand it. It identifies areas of behavior we address in the family as well as a code of conduct outside the family. Every family needs a family mission statement. It will rally support and help to keep the family in the direction God is calling you to go.

Our family mission statement still needs to be updated but we have included it below just to give you an idea of what it is. By having a family mission statement, we are encouraging our children to rally and support one another. It also gives them a sense of direction, unity, and community. There is no one way to write a mission statement as long as it inspires your family. Write a family mission statement, prayerfully considering the direction whether it be evangelical, worship, teaching, healing.

This mission statement should be an outgrowth of your prayer time as you are seeking God for the direction of your family.

Our mission statement stresses those character qualities we would like family members to work on. We are currently working on a new one that is more reflective of our ministry and teaching outreach.

> **Our Family Mission Statement:**
> We will love the LORD,
> our God Jesus Him Only will we *serve*.
>
> We will Build Each Other
> and serve each other with *respect*.
>
> Selfishness does not exist.
> We give and respond to one another in *love*.
>
> Strife does not live here.
> We are a household established on *peace*.
>
> Our ways reflect God's thoughts.
> We are examples of His *righteousness*.

The italicized words were concepts we impressed upon our children even when they were toddlers. Your mission statement should be meaningful to your family. You may want your kids to contribute to it. Your mission statement is most effective if it has meaning for everyone in your home. Now that our children are older we have changed our mission statement.

19
Family Flag

> The men said to her, "This oath you made us swear will not be binding on us unless, when we enter the land, you have tied this scarlet cord in the window through which you let us down, and unless you have brought your father and mother, your brothers and all your family into your house.
> - Joshua 2:17-18 (NIV)

The scarlet cord represented the salvation of Rahab's household. It was a visual representation of the oath made between her and the spies Joshua sent to spy the land. Visual presentations can be powerful. God told Abraham to look at the stars when he promised to make him the father of many nations. (Genesis 15:5) I have found a fun way to show our allegiance to the LORD Jesus and at the same time spend quality time with my children. Just as our country has a flag, our family has a flag.

We made a family flag some time ago when our children were young. Ours is very simple. It is a simple flag with a heart in the middle with five silver stars for each member of the family. The heart is encased in blue symbolizing our heavenly connection with the LORD. It is on a white background emphasizing our purity of heart towards the Lord Jesus. The process of making the flag was fun. The kids were all preschoolers at the time and yet they still remember coloring the flag and pasting aluminum foil stars on the poster paper.

The flag generally hangs in our basement which was our family gathering room. You may decide what character qualities you want to emphasize before you design your flag. Actually hanging the flag up helps to solidify the experience for the kids and builds family unity especially if each one contributed to the making of the flag. The process of everyone making the flag will be messy but that is what makes it so much fun. Allow the mess to be made because it is all part of the process.

20
Review Family Photo Album

> I will remember my covenant with Jacob and my covenant with Isaac and my covenant with Abraham, and I will remember the land.
> - Leviticus 26:42 (NIV)

God remembers His promises. He is the God of Abraham, Isaac and Jacob and He indeed will be the God of our children as He is our God. We have to plan times of remembrance with our children about their godly heritage. A photo album with recorded events is the perfect way to review your spiritual heritage with your child. Review the photo album with your children and reminisce with them. I am the photographer in our family and I like to document our family visually. I regularly display the photographs to the kids and others so that we may enjoy them.

I also like videotaping not just special events but everyday family life. When reviewing the images we can encourage our children to view photographs with fond memories. We plan regular times to go through the photo albums. My children have their own photo albums that they put their favorite snap shots in so they can look at them even when I am not around. They often ask for the duplicate pictures for their photo albums.

It is also a good idea to get magazines that have lots of pictures and books of prominent Christian leaders. Our children have read old writings of Frederick Douglass, Phyllis Wheatley and also biographies of prominent missionaries. Pictures can also be posted at home.

21
Rites of Passage

> Brace yourself like a man; I will question you, and you shall answer me.
> - Job 38:3 (NIV)

God tells Job to brace himself like a man. Clearly, God has an expectation from us a men and all humankind. The children of Israel marked manhood from age 13- 20. In Israel young men could own land but could not sell it until twenty-one. The transitional years biblically appear to be between thirteen and twenty. We have to prepare our children for adulthood.

In our family we have to mark a coming of age or officially becoming an adult. In our family I try to transition our teen family members into adults by giving them more responsibility and opportunities for independence. My wife likes the fact that our children are given more mature household tasks such as mowing the lawn, doing laundry, or planning a family event. I think the time a child transitions to young adulthood needs to be marked with a party or some kind of memorable ceremony.

Ceremony does not mean a lot of people need to come over but it does need to be significantly marked. In the Rites of Passage in our family I review with the young person how to financially handle money including balancing a checkbook and creating and maintaining a budget. It also includes taking responsibility for spiritual maturity such as doing a missionary trip or giving time and energy to a worthy cause.

We also give our children purity rings once we "have the talk" with them. It is important that our sons and daughters recognize the power of purity. The ring is a symbol of their allegiance to God, parents and their future mate. I also have Christian adults and trusting, extended family members write letters to your kids or declare (speak over them in a ceremony) the positive qualities they would like to see our young people develop.

My wife and I pray and give our transitioning children a symbol of our love and commitment to them in their new phrase of life as we move from their parents essentially telling them what to do to their advisors. Every parent has to make that transition to have a healthy relationship with their adult children.

22
Planning A Family Trip

> He said to his servants, "Stay here with the donkey while I and the boy go over there. We will worship and then we will come back to you."
> - Genesis 22:5 (NIV)

It seems obvious from this Scripture that Abraham and Isaac enjoyed worshipping as a family and taking a trip was a natural part of this family or culture. Most of us take family vacations, but do we take vacations as a family for spiritual rejuvenation? It is important that we go alone with our family to places of worship or solace. There are many Christian camps, retreats, etc. that provide ministry to families. When you are not in your regular surroundings, you will find you connect better with your child. I think those of us in urban areas need to really make this a priority in our lives.

If you cannot do a whole day you can place a day's retreat. Since my children are home educated, I occasionally take off a day or so to take the family on a real field trip. These trips are fun. I know all of us cannot take the day off but when you do it is great. Trips build fond memories and the kids like planning the trip with me. You can also plan trips on the weekends or make special trips after work. We do not live far from the beach. Occasionally, after work we will go to the beach with the kids.

Trips can be very simple and inexpensive. You may check your local newspaper for family friendly attractions in your area.

It is important that we provide our children with the opportunity to know God for themselves. Getting away specifically for this purpose cements in our children's hearts how important it is to seek God regularly. It also establishes the habit of regularly seeking God as an adult. Often times in Scripture God spoke to individuals when they were alone. Our children will be impacted when they begin to understand they can seek God for themselves.

23
Family Song

> Kenaniah the head Levite was in charge of the singing; that was his responsibility because he was skillful at it.
> - 1 Chronicles 15:22 (NIV)

I may not be skillful at singing but I do enjoy singing. It is a great way for families to bond even if you are not a gifted singer. Songs hold a special place in history. As most of you know spirituals were songs in code used to secure freedom. It was very creative way to communicate. There is something special about music that binds people together. Although your musical taste may be different from your children's, you can have fun taking songs they enjoy and changing the lyrics to reflect your Christian values. I have also had my kids make up new stanzas for well known songs reflecting our values. It is a lot of fun.

You can also make a family song if you are musical, or change a well known song into a family song. Or like us you may ascribe certain songs to your family. We have certain songs which remind us of when our children were dedicated and key events in our lives.

Music really stirs up memories. Children in particular are musically oriented and remember lyrics very easily. They are apt to connect with us by humming or singing a song.

By the way, children can learn almost anything if you set it to music. It can become a fun way to review homework or schoolwork if you teach them rudimentary facts, like setting the multiplication table to music. If you add movement they will probably remember it even more. If you play a musical instrument or are in any way musically inclined you are ahead of me in this area.

24
Arts and Crafts

> Then Moses said to the Israelites, "See, the LORD has chosen Bezalel son of Uri, the son of Hur, of the tribe of Judah, and he has filled him with the Spirit of God, with skill, ability and knowledge in all kinds of crafts...He has filled them with skill to do all kinds of work as craftsmen, designers, embroiderers in blue, purple and scarlet yarn and fine linen, and weavers—all of them master craftsmen and designers.
> - Exodus 35:30-31: 35

It is clear from this Scripture that God gives gifts and talents to individuals and families to bless others. The above Scripture illustrates this point. We all have talents and abilities and any men, perhaps because Jesus was a carpenter draw particular delight from making things with their hands.

I am not as creative as my wife when it comes to arts and crafts. Generally, I encourage the kids to come to me with their ideas. You may also get simple crafts books from your library. It is great to do paint or messy arts and crafts projects outside or on days when you are washing the car and you can easily wash away the paint. Kids will remember times of creative play and will have the craft mementoes to reference the memorable occasion. Getting messy with your children really cements memories for them. Be careful that you get nontoxic craft materials for young children.

I note some fun projects in the Appendix you can do with children of various ages. Working towards a tangible goal like completing a project helps you to work on problem-solving skills. Remember you are not so much interested in the completed project as you are in the process. Working on a project builds skills to work on more important projects.

Psychologists often place people in conflict together to complete a common arduous task. Defenses usually fall and people bond when they successfully solve problems together.

25
Do a Family Budget

> Suppose one of you wants to build a tower. Will he not first sit down and estimate the cost to see if he has enough money to complete it?
> - Luke 14:28 (NIV)

Sometimes as dads we make a lot of plans but fail to really plan. One of the areas we sometimes do not plan for is in the area of our finances. In the early years of our marriage I resisted making a budget because I knew our outgo exceeded our income. I did not consciously resist making a budget but I noticed whenever I would start to look at the finances a convenient excuse would arise as to why I could not budget. It took a while but one day this Scripture jumped out at me.

I had to plan for my family financially because most of our family decisions are financially based. You don't take your child to the amusement park because the price of the admission ticket is prohibitive. You miss out on a church family trip because the price of the tickets is too high. Your children do not necessarily understand why they are being denied a treat. This can create resentment. I have also worked with dads who think they don't have the money for the amusement park tickets only to find out if they give up a few nights of bowling they would have the funds for their children. We have to budget with our families in mind.

We need to do budgets. Budgets must also accommodate our children's interests. Since we are a home-schooling family I always make sure my wife has adequate resources to get needed school supplies. By having a budget for that I communicate to her and the kids the importance of having good academic resources for our family. They know it is important to me and essentially I put my money where my heart is. Unfortunately, we do not have an unlimited budget but we do have something in place so that we can plan for our children's education.

Dads, what we spend money on indicates where our hearts are. We may deny it but if we are not making provisions for our family we have to reassess our values. This is not to suggest you go in debt to answer your children's every whim. It is just that you plan for their activities and interests.

26
Develop A Family Hobby Or Activity

> It is the Levites who are to do the work at the Tent of Meeting and bear the responsibility for offenses against it. This is a lasting ordinance for the generations to come. They will receive no inheritance among the Israelites.
> - Numbers 18:23 (NIV)

In the Old Testament when we read about the Levities we find that they were a family who served the LORD God and the children of Israel. If you were born in the Levite family you did not go in the wilderness and seek God's will for your life you knew you would one day serve in the temple of God. Throughout Scripture God gifts certain families with skills and gifts. These gifts fulfill the people who possess them and serve their generation.

Families overall tend to have similar interests but all too often we do not capitalize our similarities because we are so busy trying to be different. There are family goals we can work on collectively. For instance, every family can work on physical goals together. Our generation is unfortunately becoming known as the couch potato generation. There are many activities such as hiking, jogging, bicycling or power walking that we can take up as a family. The key is to pair many of our goals with spending time with our families. You can even get your church family involved.

Our kids challenge other families in our church to bowling tournaments and cycling races. Quite frankly, it is the competition that drives me but we do have fun in the process. We know another family that regularly participates in community runs and triathlons because the das is charged by the competition. As a result that family is very healthy. This same family planned a trip to the Grand Canyon and trained for a year by locally hiking.

27
Get Rid of Time Wasters

> Teach us to number our days aright, that we may gain a heart of wisdom.
> - Psalm 90:12 (NIV)

This psalm was written by Moses. Moses is an interesting character because he spent 40 years in the desert after fleeing Egypt, some say running from the will of God. Perhaps when I meet Moses on the plains of eternity I might ask him what he thinks about that. At any rate he says, "teach us." Clearly Moses understood it was a process managing our time. We have to look at our schedules daily.

Sometimes we think we will have time for our children tomorrow only to find tomorrow again our time is stolen away in other pursuits.

The word number in this Psalm is derived from the word manah. It means to organize or allot. Moses was asking God to teach him to organize his days so that he could gain a heart of wisdom. Wisdom is simply doing the right thing at the right time.

Moses wanted his life and the lives of the children of Israel he was leading to have value, significance and meaning. He wanted them to be wise. It is interesting that Moses who spent forty years in the desert would ask this of God. Perhaps he understood wasted time more than anyone else.

To better organize our days we have to identify the time wasters in our lives. Excessive television watching is a waste of time. Just staring at an animated screen does not promote family togetherness because you are not interacting with one another. Instead opt to get educational or character videos and have family discussions before and after video viewing. We like to read a book together then get it on video. This keeps us talking to one another and really spending quality time together connecting as a family.

Other time wasters include church activities. I know you are saying how dare I call church activities a time waster. Many of us dads are finding validation in our church service because we are seen and get accolades from others whereas when we are home with our children we may get a hug or a thanks dad and that kind of affirmation is just not seen as valuable for us. I'm just like you I like to make progress and be acknowledged for my achievements but my time with my kids is more valuable than a church activity. I once heard a divorced pastor say God called him to be a pastor not a husband and father therefore he was justified in leaving his family. Nothing can be further from the truth.

God considers the home the proving ground for ministry. He says that our homes must be in order before we serve in the church. God is not looking for perfect families he is looking for men to confess their sin and commit to the right way when they fall. A mistake does not disqualify you from leadership, only a failure to repent.

I am not saying do not participate in church activities or responsibilities. I am merely suggesting you monitor the time you are spending in all activities outside the home and that includes the church.

28
Learn a New Skill With Your Child

> The number of those who ate was about five thousand men, besides women and children.
> - Matthew 14:21 (NIV)

When Jesus fed the multitude there were men, women and children present. Why were children present? They were there because they were listening to the teachings of Jesus. Children were right there when Jesus was teaching. They were learning there right beside the adults.

You can learn a new skill such as a foreign language with your child. Even money management skills that you may be reading about and applying can be taught to children. Teaching a skill to your children also will solidify the skills you are learning yourself and brings your child into your adult world.

I have found even when preparing for teaching biblical messages to adults that they are more effective after I taught them to my kids first. My kids are also my best critics because they will always point out any parts of my message that are unclear to them. They are actually quite insightful. Today we have a big push for children's ministry but Jesus taught men, women and children at the same time.

Do not under estimate your child's level of understanding biblical truths.

When you learn a new skill with your child you teach them diligence and model a positive attitude. I steer away from my son's algebra but I do enjoy learning how to operate new software along with him. My daughter also taught me how to ride a skateboard. There are so many fun things you can learn with your children.

29
Listen To Your Children

> He will call upon me, and I will answer him; I will be with him in trouble, I will deliver him and honor him.
> - Psalm 91:15

God promises to always listen to us. We can call upon Him when we are upset, hurt or confused and He will always answer us. God has a ready ear to hear us. We must develop that same ear with our children. It is a given we should listen to our children but we should especially make an effort to listen to them when they are in trouble or distress. It is not a time to lecture our children when they have made a mistake. We have to initially resist the urge to say, "I told you so" until they are given ample time to recover from a mistake or bad occurrence as the result of a poor choice.

Simply listening to your children goes a long way. It is easy to come into a room when the kids are bickering and yell "Quiet!" I have learned this is not fair to my children. They are involved in an emotionally charged disagreement and must be guided to release their frustrations. This is not easy for me when I am tired and just want quiet. However, I have found when I take the time to listen to my children, it lessens these conflicts.

I really have found that if I look my children in the eye then give reassuring nods and empathize with their feelings that I gain their hearts. Most times children just want to be validated. Once their feelings are validated and their thoughts discussed then they will generally calm down significantly. It does not come to me naturally to listen to my children but through prayer and the power of the spirit of God.

I am learning how to reprogram my response to listen first then respond to their conflict. In that way dad is becoming a listening ear and they know their heavenly Father will always listen to them.

31
Wrestle With Your Kids

> So Jacob was left alone, and a man wrestled with him till daybreak. When the man saw that he could not overpower him, he touched the socket of Jacob's hip so that his hip was wrenched as he wrestled with the man. Then the man said, "Let me go, for it is daybreak."
> But Jacob replied, "I will not let you go unless you bless me."
> - Genesis 32:24-26 (NIV)

Jacob wrestled all night and it changed him. At times I think we get so spiritual we forget God has given us earthly bodies and there is much we can learn in the flesh. In this Scripture Jacob wrestles all night and comes to know God differently or a different aspect of God. Wrestling is great as it gets out our energy and is a fun way to create memories with kids. I do have the tendency to go a little overboard so I have established some family rules to keep everyone safe.

Kids need rough housing. The physical activity releases stress and it is a simple way to make a memorable moment. This comes very easy for me. I just caution you to stop when your kids have had enough or as my wife tells me before they start crying. Wrestling is something many of us do instinctually. When we are distracted then we just have to remind ourselves that this is a real memory for our children.

31
Have a Getaway Weekend

> There was a certain man from Ramathaim, a Zuphite from the hill country of Ephraim, whose name was Elkanah son of Jeroham, the son of Elihu, the son of Tohu, the son of Zuph, an Ephraimite. He had two wives; one was called Hannah and the other Peninnah. Peninnah had children, but Hannah had none. Year after year this man went up from his town to worship and sacrifice to the LORD Almighty at Shiloh, where Hophni and Phinehas, the two sons of Eli, were priests of the LORD. Whenever the day came for Elkanah to sacrifice, he would give portions of the meat to his wife Peninnah and to all her sons and daughters. But to Hannah he gave a double portion because he loved her, and the LORD had closed her womb. And because the LORD had closed her womb, her rival kept provoking her in order to irritate her. This went on year after year. Whenever Hannah went up to the house of the LORD, her rival provoked her till she wept and would not eat.
> - 1 Samuel 1:1-7 (NIV)

I was looking at the story and I find it interesting that every year Elkanah took his family on a pilgrimage to worship God. We know even the children went along. It was an annual event. It is important to get away with our families and commune with the lord.

I like going on inexpensive Christian retreats and taking individual children. It gives the kids the freedom to roam around a bit since we keep careful eyes on them at home. It is also a time to really connect with dad and make some memories. Many Christian retreats also offer family weekends and activities. I like to go at times when there are not a lot of activities planned because it gives the kids an opportunity to set the pace for the weekend.

32
Cook a Meal with Your Children

> Then he said, "My son, bring me some of your game to eat, so that I may give you my blessing." Jacob brought it to him and he ate; and he brought some wine and he drank. Then his father Isaac said to him, "Come here, my son, and kiss me." So he went to him and kissed him. When Isaac caught the smell of his clothes, he blessed him and said, "Ah, the smell of my son is like the smell of a field that the LORD has blessed.
> - Genesis 27:25-27

Isaac in his old age remembered Esau's cooking. Clearly, there appeared to be a connection between the two of them around food. There is something special about preparing a meal together then eating it. It is fellowship. Even Jesus took the time to have a meal with his disciples before he went to the cross.

Food has a way of bonding people together. Culturally many of us remember the big home cooked Sunday meals. Food has a way of creating memories.

Cooking a meal with your children is fun and reinforces your habits. If you do not know how to cook, then it is a great opportunity to learn together. Once you cook a meal with the kids, allow them to cook it by themselves. They will remember the cooking times and you will be teaching them a life skill. In addition, your wife will enjoy not having to cook for two days and it will give you extra points with your wife too. Be sure to tell the kids that cleanup is part of cooking the meal.

Here is a website for some recipes you can make with your child. http://www.easy-kids-recipes.com/easy-recipes.html

No Bake Cookies
1 stick margarine
2 cups sugar
½ cup milk
½ cup cocoa
1tsp vanilla
½ cup peanut butter
3 ½ cups of oats
Cookie sheet
Large saucepan

Directions:
- Cover cookie sheet with wax paper
- Combine margarine, sugar, milk and cocoa powder in a large sauce pan
- Boil Over medium heat bring contents to a full rolling boil
- Remove pan from heat and stir in vanilla, , peanut butter and quick oats

- Place spoonfuls of mixture onto cookie sheet. Let cookies stand until room temperature. Eat and enjoy.

Pizza
Pizza dough (easily found in frozen section of grocer)
Spaghetti sauce
Grated mozzarella cheese

Directions:
- Preheat oven to 350 degrees.
- Place on cookie sheet or pizza tin
- Pour on spaghetti sauce.
- Top with mozzarella cheese and other toppings as desired.
- Heat until cheese melts and crust is light brown

33
Use Questions

> Solomon answered all her questions; nothing was too hard for the king to explain to her.
> - 1 Kings 10:3 (NIV)

Questions are a great way to provoke thought and get your kids to be active thinkers. Ask your kids lots of questions before you leave for work. I sometimes write questions on our family bulletin board before I leave for work. For instance, I might ask my children, how many different animals can you find in the Bible? Sometimes I don't know the answer to the questions myself but I enjoy seeing what they will come up with in response to my queries. Asking for their thoughts shows you give value to their opinions and thus them as individuals. Children are unable to separate their thoughts from themselves. They appreciate you giving value to their thoughts. Those warm feelings are timeless for your children.

Really Silly Questions to Ask Your Kids
- What Bible character would you want to be today and why? What character do you think I want to be today?
- Can you find a dinosaur in the Bible? (Hint: Look in the Book of Job.)
- What was the best gift you ever received? What is the best gift you ever gave anyone?

- How old were you when you were first born? (This is not as obvious as it seems, read Jer. 1:5)
- Why do you do what you don't want to do when you really don't want to do it? (Scriptural discussion of Rom. 7:15-17 and the wording keeps the kids scratching their heads)
- What president never rode a horse but was associated with the frontier? (President Kennedy's New Frontier)
- Can you find a talking animal in the bible? (Numbers 22:30)
- If you could rename yourself reflecting, what God may be calling you to do, what would be your name? (insightful question for your children)
- What is a bandalore? Add to the intrigue by telling them they have one in their bedroom now. (Prior to 1928 yoyo's were called bandalores.)
- How many people wrote the Bible? (Great debate 40 people, inspired by one God).
- What is the longest chapter in the Bible? (Psa. 119)
- What is the most popular Hot Wheels car? (the Corvette)
- Which coin has the most ridges? (a dime has 118)
- What is your favorite color? What is most people's favorite color? (According to Crayola, most Americans favor blue)

- Can you guess where the biggest church in the world is? (The world's largest church is located in Yamoussoukro, which is the capital of Cote d'Ivoire, Africa)
- How long did the Hundred Year War last? (116 years)
- Who was the first African American to win a Nobel Peace Prize? (Ralph J. Bunche in 1950)
- How much does it cost to make a twenty-dollar bill? (Every U.S. bill regardless of denomination costs just 4 cents to make.)
- How many years is one billion seconds? (32 years)
- Why do you think God gave turtles a shell? Do you sometimes feel like a turtle? (sparks conversation)

- **Questions to Ask Kids**
- What Bible character do you identify with and why?
- What is your favorite Bible story?
- If you could live anywhere in the world, where would it be and why?
- What is your favorite color?
- What is your favorite subject in school? Why?
- Tell me about your most favorite day of the week?
- What is your favorite toy? Or game?
- What was the best gift you ever received?
- What are you most afraid of?
- What is the best Bible story you ever read?
- What do you like to think about?
- Can you write me a poem about you?

- What makes you really unique?
- What is your favorite time of the day?
- Can you draw me a picture of the family doing something you like to do?
- What would you do if you had a millionaire dollars?
- What is your favorite article of clothing?
- Do you have any special or hidden secrets?
- What do you like to talk to God about?
- What do you pray about often?
- What do you want to do when you grow up?
- What do you think about almost every day?
- What is the nicest thing someone has ever done for you?
- What is the meanest thing someone has done to you?
- What is the scariest thing that ever happened to you?
- What was your most favorite thing you did this summer?
- What is your most favorite thing you did this winter?
- What do you wish you could learn quickly? Why?
- Who is your best friend? Why?
- What do you look for in a friend?
- Describe your perfect day. What would you do? Where would you go?
- What is your favorite book? Why?
- What really bothers you?
- What is your favorite toy and why?

- What would you like to do when you get older?
- What would you do with a million dollars?
- If you make an invention to help humankind, what would you make?
- If you could spend a day doing anything you wanted, what would you do?
- What was your most embarrassing moment?
- Who do you admire?

34
Teach Conflict Resolution Skills

> A fool finds no pleasure in understanding but delights in airing his own opinions.
> - Proverbs 18:2 (NIV)

This Scripture is the heart of much disagreement. Try to get your children to engage in conflict resolution skills with one another when they are young. It is not enough to require a young child to say sorry. Saying sorry becomes words they just parrot -- each child must ask for her siblings' forgiveness and offer an olive branch or solution for the wrong done to the sibling. This may sound trite but if you start working with kids on conflict resolution when they are young you will see results.

Many teenagers do not know how to respectfully disagree with their parents because they were never taught biblical conflict resolution. I could probably write a whole book on this subject alone. Suffice to say we should not merely ignore squabbles.

Grudges have a way of festering over the years.
Do not dismiss any problem they may have, no matter how small it seems. Generally, I will ask the child to tell me what the real problem is and then we

pray about it and work it out together. Major arguments with siblings are bought to me individually and then presented at a family meeting if we are unable to resolve the conflict between the two parties. Few disagreements have advanced to the family meeting stage, because we operate under the Biblical principle of reconciliation between parties first. We have taught our children peacemaking and conflict resolution skills.

They do not always cooperate with the rules but they do have an anchor on which to draw. This life skill connects them with the teacher even when I am not present. We have used the "Young Peacemaker" by Corlette Sande.

35
Surprise Them

> Many curry favor with a ruler, and everyone is the friend of a man who gives gifts.
> - Proverbs 19:6

I do not give gifts to become a friend of my kids in the way we think of a friend but I do give gifts to capture their hearts. It also has cultivated in them a gladness to see me they never know if I am bringing them. I do not give expensive gifts but small token gifts that let them know I was thinking about them while I was at work.

I like to keep my kids on their toes so I am always surprising them. Sometimes I bring home small gifts from the office. I also like surprising them by helping them clean their room or doing a chore too. In this they learn that I genuinely care about them and value them. Yes, I discipline and lay down the law but at times I am ready to get my hands dirty to help them like Christ who left eternity and became humanity to redeem us. I dish out mercy and judgment. It is my hope that my children do not see me just as judge but a person who loves them and will kneel down to love them. Like Jesus wiping the disciples' feet I teach them that leadership is really serving others.

36
Give Rewards

> If you are wise, your wisdom will **reward** you;
> if you are a mocker, you alone will suffer."
> - Proverbs 9:12 (NIV)

I reward my kids for character traits I see in them that is making them wise. When I see an older sibling being patient with a younger sibling or when I see that they are working together on a project without arguing or when I see them show mercy or are respectful at a time when I or my wife is correcting them and yet they maintain a good attitude I give them a reward.

You can make certificates on the computer or purchase stickers at an inexpensive gift store. I like to give out character awards at our Family Meetings or Family Chapels.

I give character or fruit of the spirit awards to our children citing the exact instance when we (either their mother or I) witnessed them exercising a particular fruit. These certificates encourage good behavior and help to encourage peace in our household. This is important because we are with one another all the time. Once a child accumulates many certificates I may treat them to something special.

37
Get Used to Repeating Yourself

> But I tell you that anyone who is angry with his brother will be subject to judgment. Again, anyone who says to his brother, 'Raca,' is answerable to the Sanhedrin. But anyone who says, 'You fool!' will be in danger of the fire of hell.
> - Matthew 5:22

This is a rather harsh verse but I wanted to point out that when Jesus said anything of importance it was worth repeating. As a father I have learned that repeating myself comes along with the job. I just keep saying it over and over again in different ways (letters, lectures, stories, videos, scripture and other people quotes). I often say the same thing over and over and pray that it sticks. I pray that they will get it one way or the other. Parenting is really a walk of faith. We relentlessly pursue our children's hearts and lead them to Christ all the while praying and hoping they are getting it. Jesus struggled with the disciples too. He repeated Himself over and over. Yet, it was not until after His resurrection that they stepped up to the challenge to really be disciples of Christ. I rest in that assurance as I keep reminding myself that it is okay to repeat myself again and again.

38
Make Contracts

> I have set my rainbow in the clouds, and it will be the sign of the covenant between me and the earth.
> - Genesis 9:13 (NIV)

God honors covenants or promises. We can do the same. Make contracts with your children. This especially works for teenagers. When you come to certain agreements together then allow your teenager to draw up a contract with you. I let my children choose their own punishment and if they do not keep up with their end of the deal on a contract. I generally let my children choose the consequences because they are immensely more severe than I would be. The contract also keeps them from arguing "but dad that's not fair." A contract is not the only preventative measure but when coupled with other measures it communicates to the child your willingness to be fair to him/her.

39
Build Family Spiritual Traditions

> "Celebrate the Feast of Unleavened Bread, because it was on this very day that I brought your divisions out of Egypt. Celebrate this day as a lasting ordinance for the generations to come.
> - Exodus 12:17 (NIV)

The Passover was important for the children of Israel to observe. God himself informed them to observe it for generations. We too should have traditions that help seal our children's identities and family cohesiveness. Family traditions keep memories alive. As first generation Christians my wife and I have adapted a great many Christian family traditions. We regularly take communion at home. We have taught our children the reality of communion so that it is just not a church tradition but a family tradition as well. We endeavor to have our Christian faith and family heritage so intertwined that our children find their identity first and foremost in being Christians. We add spiritual significance to all the holidays. It is my desire that these traditions live in future generations when I am long since gone.

40
Start a Family Business

> At that time the LORD set apart the tribe of Levi to carry the ark of the covenant of the LORD, to stand before the LORD to minister and to pronounce blessings in his name, as they still do today.
> -Deuteronomy 10:8 (NIV)

Every family has a call of God on it. Scripture illustrates how God would call whole families. For instance the tribe of Levi was called to the priesthood. It was generally accepted anyone born into that lineage would serve in the temple.

Families today are no different. Some are called to be missionaries, others are called to the ministry of helps and still others to leadership. Pray about a cause your family can get behind and work collectively towards it. We minister to families and travel quite a bit to home school conventions and family conferences and generally involve our children in the planning. They also work the book table and keep inventory.

This is part of our family's call right now. They are also encouraged to share their insight and solutions to any problems we may encounter. They are quite creative in their approach and we have implemented some of their suggestions. This can be done in a family business as well as ministry. In addition, money management and problem solving skills may be worked on together. You really connect with kids when you brainstorm business solutions together.

41
Plan a Family Night

> Plans fail for lack of counsel, but with many advisers they succeed.
> - Proverbs 15:22 (NIV)

As you probably already know it is imperative that you plan very deliberately to have leisure time with your family. Counsel with your calendar and put other commitments on the back burner to give your family at least one night of uninterrupted fun at home. Family Nights are important. You should plan to give yourself one hundred percent to your family when you are home. Put Family Night on your calendar and do not plan any meetings or work late on those nights. By having at least one night a week scheduled to be home you can juggle your work and ministry commitments. A dad who worked as a lawyer said that he keeps one night totally devoted to his family because he knows the nature of his office is that each week he will inevitably have to do overtime. Therefore, he schedules one night a week as family time and refuses to schedule clients, meetings or to make any deadlines that night. This communicates your love and commitment to your family.

42
Hire Out When You Can

> Wisdom is supreme; therefore get wisdom. Though it **cost** all you have, get understanding.
> - Proverbs 4:7

Time is really not money. You can get money back, but you cannot get your time back. We have to think wisely and not be so caught up in money that we do not make wise decisions. Sometimes we dads in the pursuit of saving money do things we can get someone else to do. For instance, when my kids were small my wife begged me to hire a lawn service so I could give up cutting and manicuring the lawn on Saturdays, so we could have some quality family time. I reluctantly did hire a lawn service. I found the time I gave to my family outweighed the cost of the lawn service. It was also nice to have a consistently manicured lawn. Of course, as my son got older I gave him that task. As dads we have to know when to give up the buck to get time.

43
Be More Efficient at Work

> Teach me to number my day that I may gain a heart of wisdom.
> - Psalm 90:12 (NIV)

Theologians tell us this Scripture is written by Moses when he roaming in the wilderness. His days were probably rather monotonous. He saw the same thing everyday. He did the same thing. He was in a rut. The word number in Hebrew is translated from the word *manah* which means organize so in essence Moses was saying to teach me to organize my life so I can be wise. My wife regularly writes and speaks on time management and she shared with me that most people can recapture almost a whole day each week just by organizing themselves. I know we should leave our job at the job but this becomes very difficult when we are disorganized at work.

I have learned when I am efficient at work that I can really leave work at work. It is only when I have loose ends that I begin to think about the office. Therefore in order to be fully present with your family when you are there you must make a decisive plan to tackle your poor time management and organization skills at work.

44
Plan Theme Nights With the Kids

> David, wearing a linen ephod, danced before the LORD with all his might,
> - 2 Samuel 6:14 (NIV)

David knew how to celebrate a victory likewise we can celebrate with our kids and make it a learning process as well. Children love to anticipate events.

Yes, they like surprises but often the fun in Christmas is lost after the gifts are open. Theme parties put kids in the planning mode and also helps them to explore and use their creativity. They will anticipate the party. You can do family meeting parties with Biblical themes like everyone being disciples. You can also do Mexican, Roman or French night at the Family Meeting and have the children surprise you with recipes and crafts from the country or time period. Be certain to be overly excited and very enthusiastic with your children.

45
Give Meaningful Goodbyes

> Then Jacob called for his sons and said: "Gather around so I can tell you what will happen to you in days to come.
> - Genesis 49:1 (NIV)

Jacob was about to crossover to eternity and as he prepared for his exit by calling all his sons together and pronouncing a blessing on them. While we may think we are just going to work or a church meeting, etc. it is important that we take the time to make the goodbye memorable for our children.

When you have to be away for extended periods of time, such as a business trip, be certain you take the time to properly say goodbye to your children. Do not sneak out the house to avoid teary farewells. You may want to leave letters or video/audio or DVD messages for the kids to listen to in your absence.

Of course, these should not replace daily telephone calls to speak to each child. I have a friend who travels a lot and thus makes silly videos of himself telling Bible stories to his kids. They like watching him over and over and those videos are a cherished family memory as the kids have gotten older. Even dads who leave daily may have a quick round robin of family prayer or decree a blessing on the family before they leave for work.

46
Bring Your Kids to Your Job

> "Come, follow me," Jesus said, "and I will make you fishers of men."
> - Matthew 4:19 (NIV)

The disciples understood the mission of Christ by being around him. Fishing for men well may have been a metaphor before the disciples actually walked with Jesus. It is often the same way with our kids.

Your kids will not understand what you do unless they get an opportunity to see it. Kids understand things concretely and visually. They need to see where you are when you are not with them. If you work at a job where it is just not feasible then provide video or pictures so your children can see where you work. They can also be encouraged to pray for you and other co-workers.

47
Let Your Children Call or Email You at Work

> Then King Rehoboam consulted the elders who had served his father Solomon during his lifetime. "How would you advise me to answer these people?" he asked. They replied, "If you will be kind to these people and please them and give them a favorable answer, they will always be your servants."
> - 2 Chronicles 10:6-7 (NIV)

We all know the story of Rehoboam. He chose to listen to the young inexperienced advisors instead of the wise elders who told him to listen to the people and respond to their questions they would have served his kingdom willingly. The people just wanted to know they had access to the king and that their needs would be addressed by him. Likewise our children need to be assured they have access to us.

Email is great and it allows you to answer your children when you get a break. If you do not have email available set a time when your kids can call you. I can get inundated with email at work but if I see it is from the kids it often will make me smile. If you travel you might try giving your child a two way radio so that the child can call you almost any time. Cell telephones with unlimited airtime might be an option for you as well.

48
Do an Interactive Journal With Your Children

> . . . "Chisel out two stone tablets like the first ones, and I will **write** on them the words that were on the first tablets, which you broke. - Exodus 34:1 (NIV)

God's written word the Bible is our record of his goodness. God stressed the importance of keeping a written record. It is something very special about writing.

This is one of my kids' favorite ways to connect with me. Each child has a notebook that they write questions to me and I answer them. Actually we both ask questions to one another. You would be surprised at the things children will be very candid with when writing about it. Their letters are just between us. They will generally answer the questions while I am at work. They then give me the notebooks before they go to bed at night. I respond to their questions while they are sleeping.
I put the notebooks either under their pillow or on the dining room table before I leave for work.

Generally we do not discuss what is written in the journal unless my children initiate such conversation. At first, we used just regular notebooks to share our thoughts but our shared writings have become so cherished that my children like to write in special journal books. You can get a jumpstart as to what questions to ask your child by looking at some of my suggested questions in the next section of this book.

Interactive journals have the added benefit of improving a child's communication skills because they have to think through their thoughts then write them out. Actually, our journals have become part of our home school curriculum. I use the journals to ask silly questions sometimes so that the kids enjoy the process and do not think everything they write has to be so weighty. You can see my list of questions at the end of this book. Asking questions makes it easier to write for children. They feel less intimidated about the whole writing process when they can do it easily.

49
Pray with Your Kids

> Then he prayed, "O LORD, God of my master Abraham, give me success today, and show kindness to my master Abraham.
> - Genesis 24:12 (NIV)

God always honors our prayers on behalf of others. This may almost seem so obvious that we may trivialize it or neglect to do it because it seems so simplistic. Nothing moves a child's heart than having you pray with them concerning their personal concerns. Regularly pray with your children as this shows your interest and keeps the lines of communication open.

Most children will never turn you down when you offer to pray with them. When you are praying with them you will get to hear their heart. Sometimes little ones may not come to you if you laugh at their requests. Give full attention to their concerns. Also the best thing about praying with your child is that you can find out what is on their hearts and sometimes be instrumental in actually answering their prayers. This is one of the best parts about being a dad—being a bridge to God for our children.

Being a bridge also means you may have those difficult conversations too—like dad why did God let grandma die? Or why did he let Billy get hit by a car. It is at these times you can correct a child's theology and secure their relationship with God.

Many blocks in our relationship with God may be traced back to childhood misunderstandings. This is especially true of children who experience trauma as children. We have to be sensitive that we may think of as a trite event may really affect a child deeply.

Praying with them regularly gives us a bit of insight into their souls.

50
Pray for Your Children

> His sons used to take turns holding feasts in their homes, and they would invite their three sisters to eat and drink with them. When a period of feasting had run its course, Job would send and have them purified. Early in the morning he would sacrifice a burnt offering for each of them, thinking, "Perhaps my children have sinned and cursed God in their hearts." This was Job's regular custom.
> - Job 1:4-5 (NIV)

Job prayed regularly for his children. It was his custom to pray for them. God referred to him as a righteous man. We should heed his actions which God deemed righteous.

God has called us to be stewards over our children. Pray that God will show you how to be effectively steward your children. We need to know how to nurture the gifts, talents, and abilities God has given our children. Our children are seeds that must be guarded and nurtured to blossom.

As we pray for them, we have to constantly have ourselves on the altar. Actually in praying for them we are actually praying for ourselves too. God is a generational God. He is the God of Abraham, Isaac and Jacob and anyone else who calls on His name. Family is important to God. It was His idea. He delights in our faith being passed down through various generations. It really brings glory and honor to God when we can mentor our children in their faith.

I like to pray the Fruits of the Spirit over my children because I find many of the character flaws in my children are the result of a particular fruit not manifesting itself in their lives. I have found this also to be a good way to pray consistently for them. In prayer, I may concentrate on a different fruit every day.

Prayer produces intimacy, I once heard someone say. I agree my praying for my children has helped me to be more receptive to them in other areas.

Prayer is foundational to everything I do for my children.

51
Form a Family Sports Team and Challenge Other Families

> Do you not know that in a race all the runners run, but only one gets the prize? Run in such a way as to get the prize. Everyone who competes in the games goes into strict training. They do it to get a crown that will not last; but we do it to get a crown that will last forever. Therefore I do not run like a man running aimlessly; I do not fight like a man beating the air. No, I beat my body and make it my slave so that after I have preached to others, I myself will not be disqualified for the prize.
> - 1 Corinthians 9:24-27 (NIV)

Engaging in sports when it is done well teaches children great life lessons. You can form your own sports team and challenge other families in your church and community. Even children who are not sports enthusiasts will enjoy time team building skills that you can reinforce.

Working as a team in a fun activity will solidify the skills you want your children to have in your absence such as: cooperating to accomplish a goal, sacrificing for the good of the group, developing strategy to win a game, covering for others' weaknesses and working as a unit. You do not necessarily want to stress winning each time because children may think you need to win at all cost. It is important to celebrate your victories as well as defeats. Go for ice cream after a game.

The competitions also do not have to be very physical either. You can participate in cup stacking competitions, indoor bowling or miniature golf at home. You can even set up a mock volleyball game by using two chairs and a beach ball. Your family could also train to run in a marathon or a triathlon where you are competing against yourself and collectively as a group. You might also sponsor a sports day at your church or in your community.

Cup stacking: http://en.wikipedia.org/wiki/Sport_stacking

52
Make a Video for Your Kids Especially When You are Away

> Like the appearance of a rainbow in the clouds on a rainy day, so was the radiance around him. This was the appearance of the likeness of the glory of the LORD. When I saw it, I fell facedown, and I heard the voice of one speaking.
> - Ezekiel 1:28 (NIV)

In the above Scripture Ezekiel sees God's likeness and is moved emotionally. Just the appearance of God, or His image our children, especially young children relish in seeing us when we are not there especially on the television screen. Young children will love to see you on television because it is a bit surreal to them. You can tell funny stories or sing silly songs so that the kids can replay it often.

It should be funny and entertaining. One dad in the military actually recorded himself singing silly songs so that his kids could sing along with him while he was away. If you make a video that will be used quite a bit be sure to make a copy of it because the kids may wear it out or lose it.

53
Raise Money with Your Kids for a Worthy Cause

> If anyone is poor among your fellow Israelites in any of the towns of the land the LORD your God is giving you, do not be hardhearted or tightfisted toward them.
> - Deuteronomy 15:7

God encourages us to be generous. You can research a cause: social, environmental, political, etc. with your children and come up with creative ways to raise funds to support that charity. You may sponsor your own car wash or do a family bake sale to support the cause. Your kids might want to set up a lemonade stand or other creative venture. As you work towards your goal, make off your progress. You may want to keep a chart on the refrigerator. The kids could also work on projects while you are at work and share it with you when you get home. Meeting the desired goal is not as important as enjoying working with one another.

Additionally, it teaches our children to be other directed. Children who have an opportunity working for others generally are more sensitive to the needs of others.

Fifty-Four
Make a Family Newspaper or Newsletter

> "Oh, that my words were recorded, that they were written on a scroll, that they were inscribed with an iron tool on lead, or engraved in rock forever!
> - Job 19:23-24 (NIV)

In this Scripture Job laments that his words are not recorded and preserved forever. Words do carry a bit of immorality when put in a permanent form.

Family newspapers and newsletters can also teach children valuable skills such as organizing, working in a group and with the ease of desktop software your children can easily make a newsletter or newspaper detailing what occurred in your absence. The project should not be tedious. Kids can draw pictures or write stories about what happened while you were at work. Those who do not like to write can just make a list of what happened while you were away. Children can also use digital cameras and freeware software. Some really creative types also make a family movie newspaper where family members are interviewed.

55
Keep Looking for More Things To Do with Your Kids

> Let us acknowledge the LORD; let us press on to acknowledge him. As surely as the sun rises, he will appear; he will come to us like the winter rains, like the spring rains that water the earth."
> - Hosea 6:3 (NIV)

The prophet Hosea speaks about pressing in this verse and we too have to continually press in to find activities to engage our children. Many times their hobbies or simply the things they enjoy can help us to find new ways to connect with them. The following are some fun and funny things dads can do with their kids. Check off the ones you might want to try with your family. Here are some random ideas that other dads have shared with me over the years.

101 Fun and Safe Things You Can Do With Kids

- Serve them breakfast in bed. Even a bowl of cereal is fun when you have it with your dad.
- Watch the sunset with them.
- Get a newspaper from the day they were born.
- Send them a card or letter.
- Interview your kids. Capture it on audio and video.
- Have flattering caricature of then drawn.
- Hide a note in the cookie jar.
- Have a family suggestion box.
- Have a scavenger hunt for special gifts.
- Make a kite then fly it.
- Create a family newsletter.
- Have a 'backward day.'
- Have a picture of the family taken in an instant photo booth.
- Hide a treat under your child's pillow.
- Leave funny notes to remind your child to do their chores.
- Have a formal family dinner.
- Have your child draw your portrait.
- Lie on the grass and study cloud formations.
- Hide a loving note in a book your child is reading.
- Build a house of cards.
- Give your children special coupons.
- Host a family member of the month award.
- Have a family show and tell.
- Send email to your children.
- Go bowling with your kids.
- Build a fort out of blankets and hide.

- Go camping in the backyard.
- Have a winter picnic in the living room.
- Go in training for a family triathlon.
- Make a video family commercial.
- Wrestle with your kids.
- Make homemade pizza.
- Memorize Scripture together.
- Play Bible charades.
- Draw pictures with the kids and let them guess what it is.
- Hide something and go on a treasure hunt.
- Clean your child's room for him/her.
- Have a backyard carnival.
- Have a water fight while washing the car.
- Plant indoor and outdoor gardens.
- Have a tickling contest.
- Go bike riding.
- Do a family finger painting.
- Make a macaroni necklace.
- Make no bake cookies.
- Make paper planes and launch them at your kids.
- Make silly putty.
- Make a snowman after shoveling the snow.
- Have family tee shirts printed.
- Race cars outside.
- Go to the library together.
- Have a pajama party in the middle of the afternoon.
- Dance a funny dance to music.
- Make board games.
- Do a woodworking craft together.

- Make a game of family kickball.
- Play soccer - modify the rules if necessary.
- Play baseball.
- Play hockey.
- Read a funny joke book together and try not to laugh.
- Make a silly story up together.
- Teach a Homeschool (or school) lesson.
- Make an answered family prayer book.
- Have a scavenger hunt.
- Make pirate hats out of old newspaper.
- Go running in the park.
- Play house with your daughters.
- Blow up balloons then release them.
- Make ring toss in the backyard.
- Play red light/green light.
- Play steal the bacon.
- Make musical instruments together. Form a family band.
- Do hula hoops with your children.
- Go to a museum.
- Go to a matinee.
- Color a picture together.
- Start a collection like stamps or rocks with your kids.
- Lie in the grass and look for shapes in clouds together.
- Cook dinner for mom with the kids.
- Make a fire in the fireplace and roast marshmallows.
- Have a family spelling bee.
- Act out a Bible story.

Having A Presence In Your Absence

- Put on a historical play.
- Interview your kids on current events and newsworthy items.
- Let your son dress up in your old clothes.
- Have a contest to see who can jump the highest.
- Get a kit and assembly a craft as a family.
- Do a family scrap book.
- Visit a historic home -- check your local newspaper.
- Have a who can hug one another the longest contest.
- Make up silly rhyming songs together.
- Skip rope with your kids.
- Make up a family worship and praise song.
- Go sledding.
- Go bird watching.
- Make a leaf collage.
- Give your child flashlights to sleep with under their pillow, and then sneak up on them.
- Take your children to the neighborhood you grew up in.
- Watch old television shows (family friendly) you watched as a kid with your kids.
- Make ice cream sundaes.
- Use the camcorder to make a family movie.

Derek G. Carter

Questions To Ask Kids

- What Bible character do you identify with and why?
- What is your favorite Bible story?
- If you could live anywhere in the world, where would it be and why?
- What is your favorite color?
- What is your favorite subject in school? Why?
- Tell me about your most favorite day of the week.
- What is your favorite toy? Or game?
- What was the best gift you ever received?
- What are you most afraid of?
- What is the best Bible story you ever read?
- What do you like to think about?
- Can you write me a poem about you?
- What makes you really unique?
- What is your favorite time of the day?
- Can you draw me a picture of the family doing something you like to do?
- What would you do if you had a million dollars?
- What is your favorite article of clothing?
- Do you have any special or hidden secrets?
- What do you like to talk to God about?
- What do you pray about often?
- What do you want to do when you grow up?
- What do you think about almost everyday?
- What is the nicest thing someone has ever done for you?
- What is the meanest thing someone has done to you?

- What is the scariest thing that ever happened to you?
- What was your most favorite thing you did this summer?
- What is your most favorite thing you did this winter?
- What do you wish you could learn quickly? Why?
- Who is your best friend? Why?
- What do you look for in a friend?
- Describe your perfect day. What would you do? Where would you go?
- What is your favorite book? Why?
- What really bothers you?
- What is your favorite toy and why?
- What would you like to do when you get older?
- What would you do with a million dollars?
- If you make an invention to help humankind, what would you make?
- If you could spend a day doing anything you wanted, what would you do?
- What was your most embarrassing moment?
- Who do you admire?

Things to Surprise Your Kids

- Notes
- Healthy snacks
- Stickers
- Awards (Computer generated)
- Coupons for time with dad (to do whatever the child wants to do)
- Hugs
- A new CD to listen to while they clean their room
- Traveling board game
- Fancy journal notebook
- Engraved name pens/pencils
- Favorite books
- Balloons
- Computer time
- Bible storybook
- Pocket toys
- Pictures in frames of you and them together
- Small photo albums
- A ride on your shoulders
- Colorful posters for their room
- A tickling match
- A DVD (movie) you can watch together
- A coupon for a daddy and me day

Other Resources

Fun Recipes

Here are some websites for some recipes you can make with your child.
www.easy-kids-recipes.com/easy-recipes.html
www.kulinarykidz.com/
www.nickjr.com/recipes/index.jhtml

Reading the Bible Through One Year (any version)

www.ewordtoday.com/year/
www.biblegateway.com/resources/readingplans/
www.bibleplan.org/

Good Books to Read to your Children

www.bookitprogram.com/parents/100greatbooks.asp
www.untrainedhousewife.com/good-books-to-read-aloud-to-8-12-year-olds
www.telegraph.co.uk/culture/books/3670594/100-books-every-child-should-read-An-introduction-by-Michael-Morpurgo.html
www.education.com/magazine/article/50-books-child-read-kindergarten/

About the Author

Derek Carter is the President of Foundations for Family Success, a ministry which serves today's fast-paced families. The ministry conducts practical workshops and seminars on marriage, parenting and families. In addition he does biblical counseling. Derek is also a freelance writer who has written on fathering issues. He is active in his local church and the homeschool community. He has a vision to see all men rise to be like Christ in their homes and is often heard to say "just like we want to be like Christ, our children should want to be like us." He has a burden to reach fathers so they can reach their children and therefore regularly speaks on marriage, parenting and home-school issues. He would like to hear your ideas for how you have a presence when you must be absent from your children. He is enthusiastic about any new ideas you would like to share with him. He and his wife have three children.

Visit www.dad123.org or FamilySuccess.org on the web.

www.ingramcontent.com/pod-product-compliance
Lightning Source LLC
LaVergne TN
LVHW051841080426
835512LV00018B/3005